PRIMARY SOURCES IN AMERICAN HISTORY

THE ALAMO
A PRIMARY SOURCE HISTORY OF THE LEGENDARY TEXAS MISSION

JANEY LEVY

rosen central
Primary Source

To T. G.

Published in 2003 by The Rosen Publishing Group, Inc.
29 East 21st Street, New York, NY 10010

First Edition

Library of Congress Cataloging-in-Publication Data

Levy, Janey.
The Alamo: a primary source history of the legendary Texas mission/Janey Levy.—
1st ed.
    p. cm. — (Primary sources in American history)
Summary: A collection of primary source materials highlights the story behind the Alamo and its place in the history of San Antonio, Texas.
Includes bibliographical references and index.
ISBN 0-8239-3681-3 (lib. bdg.)
1. Alamo (San Antonio, Tex.)—History—Sources—Juvenile literature. 2. Alamo (San Antonio, Tex.)—Siege, 1836—Sources—Juvenile literature. 3. San Antonio (Tex.)—History—Sources—Juvenile literature. [1. Alamo (San Antonio, Tex.)—History—Sources. 2. Alamo (San Antonio, Tex.)—Siege, 1836—Sources. 3. San Antonio (Tex.)—History—Sources.]
I. Title. II. Series.
F394.S2118 A4344 2003
976.4'03—dc21

                                       2002002368

Manufactured in the United States of America

# CONTENTS

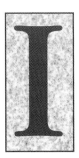NTRODUCTION

Long before the first Europeans came to North America, Native Americans inhabited the land that is now the state of Texas. The Apache arrived sometime between the years AD 1000 and 1400. The Comanche were there by the early 1700s. Less familiar groups such as the Caddo, Tonkawa, and Karankawa also lived in the region.

THE FIRST SETTLERS AND EXPLORERS

The first European to reach the area was the Spanish captain Alonso Álvarez de Pineda, who sailed along the coast of what is now called the Gulf of Mexico in 1519. Nine years later, a shipwrecked Spaniard named Cabeza de Vaca explored the interior regions. He kept a journal of his experiences and published it in Spain in 1542 under the name *Los Naufragios* (The shipwrecked men). In his journal, he described the land, the plant and animal life, and the various native peoples he had encountered. Regardless, Cabeza de Vaca's journal failed to provoke curiosity about the area. For the next century and a half, European explorers concerned themselves with other parts of the New World and paid no attention to this region.

In 1685, the Spanish suddenly became interested in the region again after the French explorer René-Robert La Salle established a colony on the Gulf Coast. The French colony lasted only five years, but its presence caused the Spanish to take action to protect their claim to the territory. Spanish soldiers and Catholic missionaries established thirty-six missions throughout the region. The missions had three purposes: to convert the Native Americans to the Catholic faith, to spread Spanish civilization in the New World, and to keep outsiders from settling in Spain's New World territories.

In 1718, Spanish soldiers and missionaries set up the fort of San Fernando de Béxar and the mission of San Antonio de Valero along the San Antonio River, in what is now the city of San Antonio, Texas. The mission's church, the building known today as the Alamo, was begun in 1744 but was never completed. Construction stopped when the upper part of the church collapsed in 1758. Then, in 1793, the Mission San Antonio de Valero was abandoned when control of it passed from the Catholic Church to the king of Spain.

A company of Spanish soldiers from Mexico moved into the mission in 1803. According to historians, this is probably when the name "Alamo" was first used for the mission. The soldiers may have named it after the Mexican village they had come from: El Alamo. Also, the mission was surrounded by cottonwood trees, and the Spanish word for cottonwood is *alamo*. Mexican soldiers occupied the Alamo until December 1835.

TIMELINE

1519 — Alonso Álvarez de Pineda is the first Spanish explorer to reach Texas.

1718 — Spanish soldiers and missionaries set up the Mission San Antonio de Valero near the San Antonio River. Apaches raid the mission often.

1793 — Mission San Antonio de Valero is abandoned.

1803 — Spanish soldiers from the Mexican village of El Alamo move into the mission, which now becomes known as the Alamo.

1821 — Mexico gains independence from Spain and grants Moses Austin permission to bring Anglo (white, non-Spanish) settlers into Texas. Moses Austin dies before he can do this.

1822 — Moses Austin's son, Stephen, carries out his father's plan.

1830 — Worried that U.S. settlers outnumber Mexicans in Texas, the Mexican government bans further Anglo settlement.

1832–1833 — Anglos in Texas complain that the Mexican government treats them unfairly. General Antonio López de Santa Anna is elected president of the Republic of Mexico.

TIMELINE

1834 ——— Santa Anna decides that Mexico is not ready for democratic rule and makes himself dictator.

1835 ——— Anglo settlers drive Mexican soldiers from the Alamo, leaving Texas under the control of the U. S. colonists.

1836 ——— Texas declares independence from Mexico. The Mexican army defeats the settlers at the Battle of the Alamo. "Remember the Alamo!" becomes the rallying cry of the Texas revolution. Texas wins its independence when it defeats Mexican forces at the Battle of San Jacinto and captures Santa Anna. It becomes the Republic of Texas.

1841 ——— The Republic of Texas returns control of the Alamo to the Catholic Church. Tourists begin to visit the site.

1846 ——— Texas becomes a state in the United States.

1883 ——— The state of Texas buys the Alamo from the Catholic Church and makes San Antonio responsible for its care.

1905 ——— The Daughters of the Republic of Texas becomes responsible for the care of the Alamo.

7

CHAPTER 1

LIFE ON MEXICO'S NORTHERN FRONTIER

By 1811, some Spanish leaders in Mexico had become unhappy with the way Spain was ruling Mexico, and they began to seek independence. Finally, in 1821, a revolution led by Agustín de Iturbide, an officer in the Spanish army, led to Mexico's independence. Iturbide then made himself president of the new nation, which included Texas. The following year, Iturbide made himself emperor. Iturbide proved to be a bad leader: he put those who did not agree with him into prison, shut down the Mexican congress, spent large amounts of money on himself, and completely ignored the unhappiness of the Mexican people.

The settlers of Texas had other problems as well. Native Americans were resentful of the Mexican settlers and often attacked the settlements. The Comanches' efforts to drive out the intruders were particularly brutal. The Comanche, who first appeared in Texas in the early 1700s, were fierce warriors. They raided settlements, stole horses, and kidnapped women and children. They also waged war against other tribes. Though their enemies feared them, the Comanche were also known for their skill as traders and for their horsemanship. Their society was democratic, and each person had great individual freedom.

The painter George Catlin preserved much information about nineteenth-century Comanche civilization. Catlin painted portraits of many Comanches in Texas, including a remarkable warrior known as the Little Spaniard (His-oo-san-ches in the Comanche language) because he was half Spanish.

In the 1834 portrait on page 10, Catlin shows the powerfully muscled Little Spaniard wearing a loincloth and moccasins that reach to his knees. The Little Spaniard carries a bow and arrows, a knife, a lance, and a shield decorated with feathers. Catlin keeps the background simple to prevent it from drawing the viewer's attention away from the Little Spaniard.

The full-length standing pose that Catlin chose for the Little Spaniard was often used for portraits of European nobles. This indicates that Catlin felt the Little Spaniard was a man of great honor who deserved respect. Catlin's own words confirm this. In a letter included in a book of his correspondence published in London, England, in 1841, the artist described the Comanche as a great warrior who also possessed "gentlemanly politeness and friendship." The Little Spaniard was, Catlin wrote, "one of the most extraordinary men at present living in these regions."

Five hundred years before the Comanche arrived, small bands of Apache moved around the region following the buffalo herds. They also raised corn, beans, pumpkins, and watermelons. Before the Comanche arrived in the early 1700s, the Apache had been the most powerful people in the region. They attacked other tribes and raided the Spanish missions, including San Antonio de Valero.

Italian artist Claudio Linati lived in Mexico from 1825 to 1827 and created a picture of an Apache *cacique*, or chief, which is shown on page 12. It is not a portrait of a particular person; instead, it shows the typical appearance of an Apache

leader. The picture is one of forty-eight hand-colored litho-graphs in a book Linati published in Brussels, Belgium, in 1828, titled *Costumes Civils, Militaires et Réligieux du Mexique* (Civilian, military, and religious dress of Mexico). In the 1700s and 1800s, Europeans were interested in the clothing worn by people around the world.

To illustrate that the Apache were great riders, Linati drew the chief sitting calmly on top of a powerful, rearing horse. The chief carries a bow and arrows, a lance, and a shield. He wears moc-casins, cotton pants, a headdress with pale green feathers, a pale blue necklace, and earrings. Red and brown designs are painted on his body. Although Linati's pictures were intended to provide spe-cific information, they are not always reliable. For example, the col-ors applied to the lithograph are not the same in all copies of the book. In a copy housed at Yale University, the headdress feathers are an intense green, the necklace is an intense blue, and the shield has no red. The shield in both pictures also lacks the feathers that normally decorated shields. Even more oddly, unlike the shield shown in the Yale University book, the shield pictured on the fol-lowing page appears to be woven like a basket rather than made of animal hide. Among tribes of the Southwest, basketry shields

George Catlin (1796–1872) painted this portrait of a Comanche warrior called the Little Spaniard in 1834, six years after he decided to devote his life to painting scenes of Native American civilization. He wanted, he wrote, to record "a dying nation, who have no historian or biographer of their own." In 1837, Catlin gathered more than 600 of his paintings of Native Americans, along with clothing and other objects, to form his North American Indian Gallery. For twelve years, he traveled around the United States and Europe exhibiting his gallery. Most of these paintings, including this portrait, are now located in the Smithsonian American Art Museum in Washington, D.C.

Pl. 22.

COSTUMES MEXICAINS.
Cacique Apache
des bords du Rio Colorado dans la Californie.

Italian Claudio Linati (1790–1832) introduced lithography to Mexico when he arrived in 1825. He set up a lithographic printing shop and trained others to make lithographs. Like many artists, Linati liked lithography because it is much like drawing on paper. To make a lithograph, the artist draws a picture on a block of limestone with a greasy crayon. The stone is then wetted. The water runs off the greasy drawing but soaks into the rest of the stone. When ink is spread across the stone, it sticks to the drawing but not to the wet areas. Paper is pressed against the stone to make the print. Hundreds of identical black-and-white pictures can be made this way. Sometimes, the artist or an assistant paints color onto the print, as was done with this illustration.

The artist's signature appears below the horse's rear hooves. The caption at the bottom reads: "Costumes mexicains. Cacique Apache des bords du Rio Colorado dans la Californie." Translated, this means "Mexican costumes. An Apache chief from the banks of the Colorado River in California." To understand the location this refers to, it's necessary to look back at history rather than at a modern map.

In the early 1800s, the name "Rio Colorado" was used for several rivers: the Canadian River, which runs through northeastern New Mexico and northwestern Texas; the Red River, which runs along the present-day border between Texas and Oklahoma; and the river that still bears this name. The reference to California is also misleading. In the early 1800s, the name was applied to an area that included much of the Southwest as well as modern-day California. The Apache, in fact, never lived in what is now the state of California. The Apache chief drawn by Linati probably lived in what is today western Texas or eastern New Mexico.

were sometimes buried with warriors. However, these shields were ceremonial, not functional. Whoever applied color to this lithograph did not have accurate information about Apache shields.

In 1749, some Apache made peace with the Spanish in a ceremony at Mission San Antonio. They agreed to become Christians in exchange for Spanish protection against the Comanche. Other Apaches, however, continued to raid the missions. After Mexico gained independence from Spain in 1821, the Mexican government signed peace treaties with all the Apache. However, even as the Mexicans and the Apache were making peace, the Comanche continued to threaten Mexican settlers in Texas.

The Mexican government found it difficult to defend against the Comanche. In 1820, Texas had only 4,000 Mexican settlers, mostly concentrated around San Antonio de Béxar (the community around the Mission San Antonio de Valero and the fort of San Fernando de Béxar), Goliad (east of San Antonio), and Nacogdoches (northeast of San Antonio, near the Louisiana border). There were too few of them to defend the vast empty spaces of Texas, and the Spanish government was unable to persuade more Mexicans to settle there. Most Mexicans thought the land in central Mexico was more valuable than the land in Texas. Finally, the Spanish government decided to allow settlers from the United States to come to Texas, hoping that these Anglo (white, non-Spanish) settlers would create a buffer zone that would help protect the Mexicans from Comanche attacks.

In 1819, Missouri entrepreneur Moses Austin was looking for an opportunity that would help him recover from recent financial setbacks. He decided that sparsely populated Texas offered great opportunities to someone who was willing to work hard. In 1820, he traveled to San Antonio to seek the Spanish governor's permission to establish a colony. Austin persuaded Governor Antonio

María Martínez to write to Commandant General Joaquín de Arredondo, recommending that Austin be permitted to carry out his plan. To secure approval, Austin gave assurance that the settlers would all be Catholic, even though this was not true. Austin also promised that the settlers would bring documents certifying their good conduct. While he waited for an answer, Austin returned to his home in Missouri. The wet, cold weather during the four-week journey left Austin with pneumonia.

In January 1821, Ambrosio María de Aldasoro, a member of Arredondo's council, wrote the letter shown on page 15 to Governor Martínez, granting Austin permission to establish his colony. When Austin received word, he immediately began preparations for the undertaking. However, the effort proved too much for him. Weakened by the pneumonia, he died in Missouri on June 10, 1821, before he could realize his dream.

On his deathbed, Moses Austin asked his wife to tell their twenty-eight-year-old son, Stephen, that his last request was that Stephen establish the Texas colony. Stephen immediately set about completing the plans for the settlers' journey to Texas. In January 1822, Stephen and 300 Missouri families settled on the fertile land between the Colorado and Brazos Rivers in southeastern Texas. Problems with the Mexican government arose immediately. When Moses Austin had received permission for the colony in 1820, it was from the Spanish government, which then controlled Mexico. The government of newly independent Mexico, headed by Agustín de Iturbide, did not recognize the Anglo settlers' right to establish a colony.

Stephen Austin traveled to Mexico City, where he persuaded the Mexican government to grant permission for his colony. Stephen also had himself named *empresario*, or administrative agent, for the colony. As empresario, he was responsible for controlling

On January 17, 1821, Ambrosio María de Aldasoro wrote to Governor Antonio Martínez, informing him that Moses Austin would be allowed to settle in Texas with 300 "Missourian" families. For a translated excerpt of this letter, see page 56. The letter is one of 250,000 manuscript pages of official Spanish and Mexican government records of Texas that are now in the Béxar Archives, located in the Center for American History at the University of Texas at Austin. The December 26, 1820, letter that Martínez wrote to Arredondo requesting permission for Austin to bring settlers also survives. In this letter, Martínez reports Austin's assurance that the settlers would all be Catholic. On February 8, 1821, Martínez wrote to Austin informing him that he would be allowed to bring settlers.

William Howard painted this portrait of Stephen F. Austin in 1833, when Austin was in Mexico City to discuss relations between his Texas colony and the Mexican government. The small painting, done in watercolor on ivory, shows Austin dressed for hunting, with rifle, powder horn, ammunition pouch, and hatchet. Beside him is his dog, Cano. Deer or antelope are visible in the distant background. The artist followed European portrait traditions. For centuries, European nobles had been portrayed in hunting costume, often with their dogs beside them. At the English court, small watercolor portraits done on ivory were very fashionable. This portrait is now in the James Perry Bryan Papers at the Center for American History at the University of Texas at Austin.

immigration into the colony, setting up the legal system, distributing land to settlers, and overseeing the building of roads, schools, sawmills, and granaries. He was also responsible for representing the settlers' interests and concerns to the Mexican government.

To ensure that the colony's lands were divided according to Mexican law, the area had to be mapped and surveyed. Austin and two surveyors, Nicholas Rightor and Horatio Chriesman, made maps of the region around 1822. A topographical map by Austin, showing the natural and man-made features of the land, appears on page 17. Austin included rivers (identified by "*Rio*" or "R."), streams (labeled "arroyo"), forests (green areas), mountains, roads (labeled "*camino*"), and settlements. He also marked where various Native American groups lived: The Lipan Apaches (Lipanes), the Comanche, the Cado (Caddo), and the Texas Indians, from whom the state got its name.

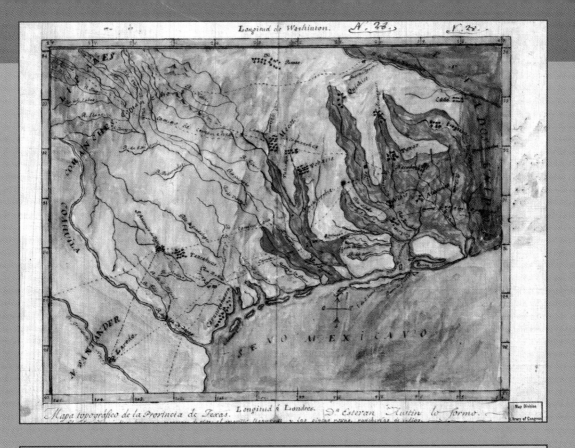

Stephen Austin probably drew this map soon after he and his settlers arrived in January 1822. It was part of his effort to gather detailed information on the colony territory prior to allocating land to the settlers. Details of the land are carefully recorded and labeled. Austin used a pen and colored inks to make the map, which is now in the collection of the Library of Congress in Washington, D.C.

The caption at the bottom of the map reads "Mapa topografico de la Provincia de Texas. Dn Estevan Austin lo formo. El color verde, indica bosques y margenes de rios; el amarillo, llanuras; y las pintas roxas, rancherias de indios." In English, this means "Topographical map of the Province of Texas. Mr. Stephen Austin made it. The color green indicates forests and river banks; yellow, prairies; and red dots, Indian settlements."

A narrow border around the map is divided into equal segments, each marked with a number. The numbers on the left and right sides are identical. Starting at the bottom, the numbers go from 27 to 34. These indicate distance from the equator, measured in degrees latitude. The numbers across the top and bottom, however, do not match. This is because they measure distance from two different points of reference. "Longitud de Washinton" (Longitude from Washington, D.C.) runs across the top, indicating that those numbers give the distance from Washington, D.C., measured in degrees longitude. "Longitud a Londres" (Longitude to London) runs across the bottom, indicating that these numbers give the distance from London, England, measured in degrees longitude.

CHAPTER 2

In spite of Stephen Austin's skillful diplomacy, tensions grew between the Anglo settlers in Texas and the Mexican government. The settlers' own actions contributed to the problems. For example, even though Moses Austin had assured Governor Martínez that the settlers were Catholics, most were in fact Protestants and refused to become Catholics. The settlers also resisted speaking Spanish and obeying Mexican laws, including the law that abolished slavery. Most settlers insisted on keeping slaves.

Soon there were more Anglo settlers in Texas than Mexicans, and many people in Mexico grew alarmed.

THE GATHERING CLOUDS OF WAR

They feared that the United States president, Andrew Jackson, and the U.S. Congress would try to claim Texas as a U.S. territory. Because of this, in 1830, the Mexican congress made it illegal for more U.S. settlers to come into Texas. To move the government of Texas closer to Mexico City and Mexican control, Texas and the state of Coahuila, which bordered Texas to the south, were combined into a single state, with its capital deep inside Coahuila.

In 1832 and 1833, Anglo settlers gathered at San Felipe de Austin to protest the Mexican government's treatment of them and to propose that Texas be recognized as a Mexican state separate from Coahuila. In 1833, Stephen Austin traveled to Mexico City to discuss the settlers' concerns with the Mexican government. The trip ended with Austin being imprisoned for more than a year by the new president, Antonio López de Santa Anna.

Santa Anna had fought alongside Agustín de Iturbide in the 1821 revolution. In 1828, he became the highest-ranking general in Mexico. His role in defeating Spain's attempt to reconquer Mexico in 1829 made him a national hero, and, in 1833, he was overwhelmingly elected president of Mexico.

In W. H. Dodd's engraved portrait on page 20, a young and handsome Santa Anna is shown on a magnificent horse. Rider and horse dominate the image, and only a sketchy background of prickly pear cactus, desert, and distant mountains places the figures in Mexico. The tradition of equestrian portraits of great leaders dates back to ancient Rome. In Santa Anna's portrait, as in many of the older equestrian portraits, the horse is well muscled, holds its head high and alert, and raises two hooves, as if anxious to gallop forward. Wind blows its mane and tail, increasing the sense of power and energy. Santa Anna calmly controls the mighty horse. The image seems to suggest that a man who can so effortlessly command the forces of nature that seem contained within the horse can certainly rule the vast territory of Mexico with equal ease.

Unfortunately, Santa Anna was as bad a leader as Iturbide had been, and his actions contributed to the tensions between Mexico and the Anglo settlers. In 1834, he declared that Mexico was not ready for democracy and named himself dictator. The following year, Santa Anna increased his control by abolishing all local governments. He became angry when anyone resisted his authority, as the Anglo settlers did, and it was this anger that caused him to throw the visiting Stephen Austin into prison. The settlers deeply resented Santa Anna's actions, which they felt took away many of their rights.

EQUESTRIAN PORTRAIT OF GENERAL SANTA ANNA.

The situation worsened in October 1835. The residents of Gonzales, a small settlement east of San Antonio, had a small cannon, which the Mexican government had given them for defense against attacks by Native Americans. In punishment for the settlers' resistance to Santa Anna's government, the Mexican army demanded that the settlers surrender the cannon. Instead, the defiant settlers fired at the Mexicans. Enraged, Santa Anna sent General Martín Perfecto de Cos and several hundred soldiers to San Antonio to disarm all Texans and arrest anyone who opposed Santa Anna. The Texas war for independence had begun.

An army of settlers led by Stephen Austin laid siege to the Mexican troops in San Antonio de Béxar. The Anglo settlers finally launched a fierce attack on Béxar on December 5, 1835. After five days of fighting, Cos surrendered and agreed to withdraw the Mexican troops and move south. About one hundred Anglo settlers then occupied the Alamo.

A diary left by José Juan Sánchez Navarro, an officer in the Mexican army, expresses their reaction to the defeat. On

W. H. Dodd engraved this undated equestrian portrait of General Santa Anna, to which color has been added by hand. Dodd engraved pictures to illustrate books, and this portrait may have been intended to go in a book. To make an engraving, the artist uses special tools to carve deep lines into a copper or steel plate. The printer then rubs ink into the lines. Paper is placed on the inked plate, and the two are rolled through a printing press under great pressure, transferring the image from the plate onto the paper. An engraved plate can be run through a press many times before the quality of the image deteriorates. This copy of the engraving is in the Center for American History at the University of Texas at Austin. Another version of this engraving, done around 1845, also exists. The poses of horse and rider are identical, but Santa Anna's simple hat has been replaced by an elaborately decorated officer's hat in the second version. The background has also been simplified. A black-and-white copy of the second version is housed in the Special Collections at the University of Texas at Arlington.

On October 17, 1835, General Martín Perfecto de Cos wrote to José Ángel Navarro, the temporary political chief in San Antonio de Béxar, calling on the citizens to defend San Antonio against the "rebel colonists." Navarro's alliance with the U.S. settlers may have prompted Cos to write Navarro this reminder of his responsibilities to Mexico. When Cos and his soldiers had reached San Antonio on October 9, Navarro had refused to allow them to use his home as their headquarters. In addition, Navarro had permitted settlers fleeing Cos to take shelter at his ranch. Cos's letter, which is a formal government communication rather than a personal exchange, is brief and to the point. Cos's large, very elaborate formal signature at the end is a reminder of his rank and authority. The letter now forms part of the Béxar Archives in the Center for American History at the University of Texas at Austin. For a translation of an excerpt of this letter, see page 56.

Vista del fuerte de San Antonio de Valero commummente llamado del Alamo tomada desde la azotea de la casa de Berumendi en la ciudad de Bexar por Jose Juan Sanchez Estrada

In elegant script below the image, José Juan Sánchez Navarro identifies the subject of the drawing and signs his name. He drew the Alamo with great care and attention to detail. The building stones and even the rope used to raise and lower the flag are visible. However, Sánchez Navarro paid no attention to the surrounding landscape. By this time, the Alamo had already assumed enormous symbolic importance in the struggle between the Texas settlers and the Mexican government, and it clearly dominated Sánchez Navarro's thoughts.

Sánchez Navarro's diary was written on the blank pages in his two-volume index to the records he kept as adjutant inspector of the Departments of Nuevo León and Tamaulipas. The index covers the period from April 1831 to November 1839. It is now in the archives of the Second Flying Company of Alamo de Parras.

December 11, 1835, two days after the surrender of the Alamo, Sánchez Navarro wrote, " 'All has been lost save honor!' I do not remember, nor am I in the mood to remember, what French king said this, perhaps under better circumstances than those in which we are today, the eleventh of December, 1835. Béxar, and perhaps Texas has been lost." Sánchez Navarro was eager for revenge, and in February 1836 he wrote in his diary that Santa Anna had granted his request to return to the war in Texas.

Sánchez Navarro left us the earliest known image of the Alamo. The above pen-and-ink drawing, done in late 1835 or early 1836,

French portrait painter Louis Antoine Collas (1775–1856) painted this miniature of Sam Houston around 1836. Like the portrait on page 16, Houston's was painted in watercolor on ivory. The tiny portrait, about three inches tall and two-and-a-half inches wide, has the oval shape favored by European nobles. It was framed and probably hung on a wall or displayed on a table. Houston sent the portrait to his longtime friend President Andrew Jackson, asking him to present it to Henrietta McEwen, the wife of Houston's cousin Robert and a friend of Jackson's as well. The portrait is now in the Sam Houston Memorial Museum at Sam Houston State University in Huntsville, Texas.

Louis Antoine Collas depicted Houston in a bust-length portrait, which means that only his head and shoulders are shown. The plain background concentrates the viewer's focus on Houston. Dressed in a military uniform, he stares directly at the viewer. The intensity of his gaze, his ruffled hair, and the fiery red cloth wrapped around his shoulders suggest that Houston is a man of great energy and purpose.

is the best record of what the mission looked like before the famous battle. It shows a complex of buildings enclosed by a high defense wall. A flag flies from the tallest building. One of the cottonwood trees that gave the mission its name stands next to the wall at the left.

While the siege of Béxar was taking place, other Texans held a meeting known as the Consultation to discuss the situation. They met in Columbia, Texas, in October, then in San Felipe in November. The Nacogdoches representative was Samuel Houston. In December 1832, Houston had settled in Nacogdoches, where he

This broadside, now in the Texas State Library and Archives, was printed by Baker and Bordens in San Felipe de Austin, as noted at the bottom of the third column. Broadsides are single sheets of paper, printed only on one side, that were meant to spread information. They were posted around town or handed out to people in town squares, taverns, and churches. They were printed as quickly and cheaply as possible, and were meant to be thrown away after they had served their purpose. As a result, copies of broadsides are rare today. A transcription of an excerpt from this broadside can be found on page 56.

quickly became a leader of the community. By October 1835, Houston was convinced that war between the settlers and Mexico was inevitable. That same month, he was appointed commander in chief for the troops of the Nacogdoches region and issued a call for volunteers. On November 12, at the Consultation in San Felipe, Houston was appointed major general of the entire Texas army.

One of Houston's first tasks as major general was to seek reinforcements for the Anglo troops occupying the Alamo. He knew that the Mexican army would attempt to retake the mission and that the small group of settlers would not be able to defend it. On December 12, 1835, only three days after the Anglo rebels had taken control of the Alamo, Houston issued a call for volunteers.

CHAPTER 3

THE ALAMO'S DEFENDERS

One man who responded to Houston's appeal for volunteers was David Crockett. Born in Tennessee in 1786, Crockett had become a legend and folk hero long before he arrived at the Alamo. He joined the Tennessee militia in 1813. Though poorly educated, Crockett became a justice of the peace in Lawrenceburg, Tennessee, in 1817. He was elected to the Tennessee legislature in 1821 and then to the U.S. House of Representatives in 1827. Crockett was defeated in his 1831 bid for reelection, but by then he had gained national fame as a sharpshooter, hunter, and storyteller. Playwright James Kirke Paulding based the hero of his play *The Lion of the West* on Crockett. A book

This lithograph was based on a portrait of David Crockett painted by Samuel Stillman Osgood (1808–1885), a sought-after portrait painter who lived in Boston. The lithograph was produced by the Philadelphia lithographic firm of Childs & Lehman. At the left, below Crockett's image, it reads "Painted by S. S. Osgood." Opposite this on the right, it reads "Childs & Lehman Litho. Philadelphia." The lithographic firm changed owners several times in the early 1800s; it operated under the name of Childs & Lehman only from 1833 through 1834, so this print must have been made during those two years. Across the bottom, in Crockett's own handwriting, it reads: "I am happy to acknowledge this to be the only correct likeness that has been taken of me. David Crockett." This copy of the lithograph is in the Center for American History at the University of Texas at Austin. The Library of Congress in Washington, D.C., also has a copy.

Painted by S.S. Osgood   On Stone.   Childs & Lehman Lith⁸ Philadelphia.

DAVID CROCKETT.

I am happy to acknowledge this to be
the only correct likeness that has been
taken of me.   David Crockett

27

based on Crockett's adventures was published in 1833. All this attention helped him win the congressional election later that year.

In 1834, *A Narrative of the Life of David Crockett of the State of Tennessee*, written by Crockett with the help of Thomas Chilton, was published. The following year, the first in a series of comic almanacs recounting outrageous tall tales about "Davy" Crockett appeared. The series continued until 1856. Crockett's *Narrative* was in part a campaign tool. The Whig party was considering him as a presidential candidate to challenge President Andrew Jackson in the 1836 election. Perhaps the lithographic portrait of Crockett shown on the preceding page was handed out as part of this political campaign. It shows Crockett, his hair neatly combed and parted, dressed as a proper gentleman of the day, in coat, vest, collar, and tie.

In the end, Crockett never ran for president. Disillusioned after he lost another bid for reelection to Congress in 1835, Crockett decided to explore Texas. If he found that it lived up to its reputation as a land full of opportunity, he would move his family there. On November 1, 1835, Crockett set out for Texas. Crockett was impressed with what he found. Texas "is the garden spot of the world," he wrote in a letter dated January 9, 1836. "I . . . have enrolled my name as a volunteer [to fight for Texas's independence] and will set out for the Rio Grand in a few days with the volunteers from the United States . . . I am in hopes of making a fortune yet for myself and family." Crockett reached San Antonio de Béxar in early February. There he met two other famous defenders of the Alamo, James Bowie and William Barret Travis.

James Bowie, born in Kentucky in 1796, was a reckless, violent man whose pursuit of wealth and adventure led him to Texas. He served as a soldier in the War of 1812, which was fought between the United States and Britain for freedom of the seas. After the

The painter of this unsigned, undated portrait of James Bowie is not known for certain. Some people believe the artist was George Peter Alexander Healy (1813–1894), though other historians have suggested it was William Edward West (1788–1857). The portrait was painted sometime between 1820 and 1836, which makes it more likely that West was the artist. Healy would have been seven in 1820 and only twenty-three in 1836, while West would have been a mature, established portraitist. After Bowie's death, the portrait went to his brother Rezin (or Reason) and passed down to his descendants. In 2001, the state of Texas purchased it at auction. It is now in the Capitol Historical Artifact Collection of the Texas State Preservation Board.

war, he was a slave trader, land speculator, and gambler. A large, physically powerful man, he was frequently involved in bloody fights. Tall tales were spread about him: He not only caught and rode wild horses, he also trapped bears and rode alligators.

The portrait of Bowie on the previous page reflects these qualities. His massive body fills the image area, testifying to his enormous strength. His face wears a severe, unfriendly look: His eyebrows are drawn together, his brow is furrowed, and his lips are clamped in a tight line. His stance seems defiant, with his arms folded across his chest and his hands clenched in fists. His right hand clutches the hilt of his American eaglehead officer's sword, which still survives. Oddly, the scabbard is not visible below his left elbow, as it should be. Perhaps the picture was damaged at some time and repainted, obscuring the scabbard.

Bowie arrived in Texas early in 1830. He married a wealthy woman and became involved in land speculation. His continuing search for wealth led him to conduct much business in Monclova, the new capital of Coahuila-Texas. When Santa Anna abolished local governments in May 1835 and ordered the arrest of foreigners doing business in Monclova, Bowie began to call for war with Mexico. He was too independent to join the regular army, but he led a small group of Texans who formed a militia, and he cooperated closely with Sam Houston.

Early in January 1836, Houston sent Bowie with thirty men to San Antonio de Béxar, with orders to destroy the Alamo. There were not enough men available to defend the Alamo, and Houston did not want the Mexican army to recapture the fort, which had become an important symbol of the Texas independence movement after the Texans drove out Cos and his soldiers. When Bowie reached the Alamo on January 19, he decided that it would be strategically important in the war for independence, and he did not follow Houston's orders to destroy the fort. When Bowie arrived at the Alamo, Colonel James C. Neill was the commander. On February 3, Bowie's old friend William Barret Travis, recently promoted to lieutenant colonel, arrived with thirty soldiers. Eight days later, Neill gave Travis command of the fort and left.

Travis, born in South Carolina in 1809, grew up in Alabama. He became an attorney, married in 1828, and settled down in Claiborne, Alabama, where he practiced law. Two years later, suspecting his wife of being unfaithful, Travis abandoned her and went to Texas, where he settled at Anahuac, on Galveston Bay, and began to learn Spanish. There were few attorneys in the area, and Travis hoped his law practice would bring him wealth.

In 1832, after being briefly imprisoned in a dispute with local authorities, Travis moved to San Felipe, where he was elected to the town council in 1834. He was appointed to lead a group of men to retake Anahuac after Mexican troops seized the town in 1835. Travis's success in this undertaking contributed to Santa Anna's decision to send General Martín Perfecto de Cos and his soldiers to occupy the Alamo. Cos called for the citizens of Texas to hand Travis over for military trial, but his demand was not met.

Travis advised the Consultation at San Felipe in November 1835 on the formation of a cavalry for the Texas army. He accepted a commission as a lieutenant colonel, and, in January 1836, Governor Henry Smith ordered Travis to take reinforcements to the Alamo. After Colonel Neill left the fort, command of the regular army troops fell to Travis, while Bowie took command of the volunteers.

Expecting the arrival of Santa Anna's troops, Travis requested additional reinforcements. Only about thirty-five men arrived, increasing the number of defenders to between 150 and 185. On

February 24, 1836, two days after Santa Anna had arrived with around 1,800 soldiers and begun the siege of the Alamo, Travis wrote a letter "To the People of Texas and all Americans in the world," pleading for volunteers. The letter is reproduced on page 33. In one of the most often quoted passages in the letter, Travis declared: "I shall never surrender or retreat. Then, I call on you in the name of Liberty, of patriotism, and everything dear to the American character, to come to our aid with all dispatch . . . If this call is neglected, I am determined to sustain myself as long as possible and die like a soldier who never forgets what is due to his own honor and that of his country—Victory or Death."

A copy of Travis's letter reached San Felipe, where the firm of Baker and Bordens printed it for distribution as a broadside. The letter was also printed in two newspapers: The *Texas Republican* printed it on March 2, 1836, and the *Telegraph & Texas Register* printed it on March 5. Hundreds of volunteers responded to Travis's plea, but none reached the Alamo in time to aid the defenders.

Captain Albert Martin carried William Barret Travis's letter from the Alamo to the small settlement of Gonzales. On February 25, 1836, Martin heard distant artillery fire and added a postscript to the letter, reporting the artillery fire and exhorting volunteers to make haste to reach the Alamo. When he reached Gonzales that afternoon, Martin turned the letter over to Lancelot Smither, who had arrived in Gonzales from the Alamo on February 24, with an estimate of the Mexican troop strength. Smither added his own postscript, again exhorting volunteers to make haste, then gave the letter to Judge Andrew Ponton, who made copies and sent them to settlements across the region. The original letter found its way back to Travis's family after Texas won its independence. In 1893, John G. Davidson, one of Travis's descendants, sold the letter to the Texas Department of Agriculture, Insurance, Statistics, and History for $85, a considerable sum of money at the time, equal to around $1,750 today. In 1909, the letter was transferred to the Texas State Library and Historical Commission, where it remains. A transcription of an excerpt from the letter can be found on page 57.

Commandancy of the Alamo—
Bejar, Feby. 24th 1836—

To the People of Texas &
all Americans in the world—

Fellow citizens & compatriots—
I am besieged, by a thousand
or more of the Mexicans under
Santa Anna—I have sustained
a continual Bombardment &
cannonade for 24 hours & have
not lost a man—The enemy
has demanded a surrender at
discretion, otherwise, the garrison
are to be put to the sword, if
the fort is taken—I have answered
the demand with a cannon
shot, & our flag still waves
proudly from the wall—I
shall never surrender or retreat.
Then, I call on you in the
name of Liberty, of patriotism &
everything dear to the American
character, to come to our aid,

CHAPTER 4

THE SIEGE AND BATTLE OF THE ALAMO

Events unfolded rapidly. On February 1, 1836, each of the fifty-four Anglo settlements in Texas elected a delegate to attend the Convention of 1836. On March 1, while the Alamo was under siege by Santa Anna and his troops, the delegates gathered in Washington-on-the-Brazos. Immediately, Convention president Richard Ellis appointed George C. Childress, James Gaines, Edward Conrad, Collin McKinney, and Bailey Hardeman to write the Texas Declaration of Independence. The next day, the declaration was submitted to the convention. Perhaps not surprisingly, it parallels the

After all the delegates signed the Texas Declaration of Independence, copies were sent to Béxar, Goliad, Nacogdoches, Brazoria, and San Felipe. By order of the convention, 1,000 copies—of which this is one—were printed as broadsides by the firm of Baker and Bordens in San Felipe de Austin. The firm's name appears in the lower right-hand corner. In the rush to get the document printed, the names of two delegates, including George C. Childress, the declaration's author, were omitted from the list of names at the bottom. These broadsides would have been distributed around the United States as well as throughout Texas. The delegates knew the Texas republic would not survive without the official recognition and support of the United States. This copy is in the Center for American History at the University of Texas at Austin. The original manuscript copy, signed by all fifty-four delegates, belongs to the Texas State Library and Archives Commission. See page 57 for a transcription of an excerpt from the declaration.

UNANIMOUS

DECLARATION OF INDEPENDENCE,

BY THE

DELEGATES OF THE PEOPLE OF TEXAS,

IN GENERAL CONVENTION,

AT THE TOWN OF WASHINGTON,

ON THE SECOND DAY OF MARCH, 1836.

When a government has ceased to protect the lives, liberty, and property of the people, from whom its legitimate powers are derived, and for the advancement of whose happiness it was instituted; and so far from being a guarantee for their inestimable and inalienable rights, becomes an instrument in the hands of evil rulers for their oppression. When the Federal Republican Constitution of their country, which they have sworn to support, no longer has a substantial existence, and the whole nature of their government has been forcibly changed, without their consent, from a restricted Federative Republic, composed of Sovereign States, to a consolidated Central Military despotism, in which every interest is disregarded but that of the army and the priesthood, both the eternal enemies of civil liberty, the ever ready minions of power, and the usual instruments of tyrants. When, long after the spirit of the constitution has departed, moderation is at length so far lost by those in power, that even the semblance of freedom is removed, and the forms themselves of the constitution discontinued, and so far from their petitions and remonstrances being regarded, the agents who bear them are thrown into dungeons, and mercenary armies sent forth to force a new government upon them at the point of the bayonet.

When, in consequence of such acts of malfeasance and abduction on the part of the government, anarchy prevails and civil society is dissolved into its original elements, in such a crisis, the first law of nature, the right of self preservation, the inherent and inalienable right of the people to appeal to first principles, and take their political affairs into their own hands in extreme cases, enjoins it as a right towards themselves and a sacred obligation to their posterity to abolish such government, and create another in its stead, calculated to rescue them from impending dangers, and to secure their welfare and happiness.

Nations, as well as individuals, are amenable for their acts to the public opinion of mankind. A statement of a part of our grievances is therefore submitted to an impartial world, in justification of the hazardous but unavoidable step now taken, of severing our political connection with the Mexican people, and assuming an independent attitude among the nations of the earth.

The Mexican Government, by its colonization laws, invited and induced the Anglo American population of Texas to colonize its wilderness under the pledged faith of a written constitution, that they should continue to enjoy that constitutional liberty and republican government to which they had been habituated in the land of their birth, the United States of America.

In this expectation they have been cruelly disappointed, inasmuch as the Mexican nation has acquiesced in the late changes made in the government by General Antonio Lopez Santa Ana, who having overturned the constitution of his country, now offers, as the cruel alternative, either to abandon our homes acquired by so many privations, or submit to the most intolerable of all tyranny, the combined despotism of the sword and the priesthood.

It hath sacrificed our welfare to the state of Coahuila, by which our interests have been continually depressed through a jealous and partial course of legislation, carried on at a far distant seat of government, by a hostile majority in an unknown tongue, and this too, notwithstanding we have petitioned in the humblest terms for the establishment of a separate state government, and have, in accordance with the provisions of the national constitution, presented to the general congress a republican constitution, which was, without a just cause, contemptuously rejected.

It incarcerated in a dungeon, for a long time, one of our citizens, for no other cause but a zealous endeavour to procure the acceptance of our constitution and the establishment of a state government.

It has failed and refused to secure, on a firm basis, the right of trial by jury, that palladium of civil liberty and only safe guarantee for the life, liberty, and property of the citizen.

It has failed to establish any public system of education, although possessed of almost boundless resources, (the public domain;) and although it is an axiom in political science, that unless a people are educated and enlightened, it is idle to expect the continuance of civil liberty, or the capacity for self government.

It has suffered the military commandants, stationed among us, to exercise arbitrary acts of oppression and tyranny, thus trampling upon the most sacred rights of the citizen, and rendering the military superior to the civil power.

It has dissolved, by force of arms, the state congress of Coahuila and Texas, and obliged our representatives to fly for their lives from the seat of government, thus depriving us of the fundamental political right of representation.

It has demanded the surrender of a number of our citizens, and ordered military detachments to seize and carry them into the interior for trial, in contempt of the civil authorities, and in defiance of the laws and the constitution.

It has made piratical attacks upon our commerce by commissioning foreign desperadoes, and authorizing them to seize our vessels and convey the property of our citizens to far distant parts for confiscation.

It denies us the right of worshipping the Almighty according to the dictates of our own conscience, by the support of a National Religion, calculated to promote the temporal interest of its human functionaries, rather than the glory of the true and living God.

It has demanded us to deliver up our arms, which are essential to our defence—the rightful property of freemen—and formidable only to tyrannical governments.

It has invaded our country both by sea and by land, with the intent to lay waste our territory, and drive us from our homes; and has now a large mercenary army advancing, to carry on against us a war of extermination.

It has, through its emmissaries, incited the merciless savage, with the tomahawk and scalping knife, to massacre the inhabitants of our defenceless frontiers.

It has been, during the whole time of our connection with it, the contemptible sport and victim of successive military revolutions, and hath continually exhibited every characteristic of a weak, corrupt, and tyrannical government.

These, and other grievances, were patiently borne by the people of Texas, until they reached that point at which forbearance ceases to be a virtue. We then took up arms in defence of the National Constitution. We appealed to our Mexican brethren for assistance; our appeal has been made in vain; though months have elapsed, no sympathetic response has yet been heard from the interior. We are therefore forced to the melancholy conclusion, that the Mexican people have acquiesced in the destruction of their liberty, and the substitution therefor of a military government; that they are unfit to be free, and incapable of self government.

The necessity of self preservation, therefore, now decrees our eternal political separation.

We, therefore, the delegates, with plenary powers, of the people of Texas, in solemn convention assembled, appealing to a candid world for the necessities of our condition, do hereby resolve and DECLARE, that our political connection with the Mexican nation has forever ended, and that the people of Texas, do now constitute a FREE, SOVEREIGN, and INDEPENDENT REPUBLIC, and are fully invested with all the rights and attributes which properly belong to independent nations; and, conscious of the rectitude of our intentions, we fearlessly and confidently commit the issue to the decision of the supreme Arbiter of the destinies of nations.

RICHARD ELLIS, *President.*

C. B. STEWART, THOMAS BARNETT.	*Austin.*	JOHN FISHER, MATT. CALDWELL.	*Gonzales.*	J. W. BUNTON, THOS. J. GAZELEY, R. M. COLEMAN.	*Mina.*	SYD. O. PENNINGTON, W. CAR'L CRAWFORD.	*Shelby.*
JAS. COLLINSWORTH, EDWIN WALLER, ASA BRIGHAM, J. S. D. BYROM.	*Brazoria.*	WILLIAM MOTLEY,	*Goliad.*			JAMES POWER, SAM. HOUSTON, DAVID THOMAS, EDWARD CONRAD, JOHN TURNER,	*Refugio.*
		L. DE ZAVALA,	*Harrisburgh.*	ROBERT POTTER, THOMAS J. RUSK, CH. S. TAYLOR, JOHN S. ROBERTS.	*Nacogdoches.*		
FRANCISCO RUIS, ANTONIO NAVARO, JESSE B. BADGETT.	*Bexar.*	STEPH. H. EVERITT, GEORGE W. SMITH.	*Jasper.*				*San Patricio.*
		ELIJAH STAPP,	*Jackson.*			B. BRIGGS GOODRICH, G. W. BARNETT, JAMES G. SWISHER, JESSE GRIMES,	*Washington.*
WILLIAM D. LACY, WILLIAM MENIFEE.	*Colorado.*	CLAIBORNE WEST, WILLIAM B. SCATES.	*Jefferson.*	ROBERT HAMILTON, COLLIN McKINNEE, ALB. H. LATTIMER.	*Red River.*		
JAMES GAINES, W. CLARK, JR.,	*Sabine.*	M. B. MENARD, A. B. HARDIN.	*Liberty.*	MARTIN PARMER, E. O. LEGRAND, STEPH. W. BLOUNT.	*San Augustin.*		
		BAILEY HARDIMAN,	*Matagorda.*				

Printed by Baker and Bordens, San Felipe de Austin.

U.S. Declaration of Independence in many ways. It begins with statements on the duties and responsibilities of government, which the Mexican government had failed to carry out, then lists specific complaints. It concludes by stating that the people of Texas had no choice but to declare Texas a free and independent republic. The declaration was unanimously approved and signed by the delegates on March 2, 1836. They then wrote a constitution for the new republic and set up a temporary government to serve until elections could be held in October.

On March 5, the twelfth day of the Alamo siege and three days after the Texas Declaration of Independence was approved, Santa Anna decided it was time to attack the Alamo. He used a map (shown on page 37) of San Antonio de Béxar and the Alamo prepared by his chief military engineer to plot the assault.

As the drama at the Alamo unfolded, attempts were made to rally volunteers beyond the borders of Texas. The broadside pictured on page 38, printed in New Orleans sometime after March 2, 1836, boldly proclaims that the handful of troops at the Alamo have driven back the Mexican army, killing or wounding 500 without suffering a single loss themselves. It goes on to state that reinforcements are headed to the Alamo and that there are enough supplies of weapons, ammunition, and provisions to guarantee the defeat of the Mexican army. The broadside was purely propaganda—none of its claims were true.

On Santa Anna's orders, his soldiers attacked the Alamo around 5:00 AM on March 6, 1836. The handful of defenders inside the fort were no match for the almost 1,800 Mexican soldiers. Fierce cannon and rifle fire from the defenders slowed the assault only briefly. As the Mexican forces swarmed into the

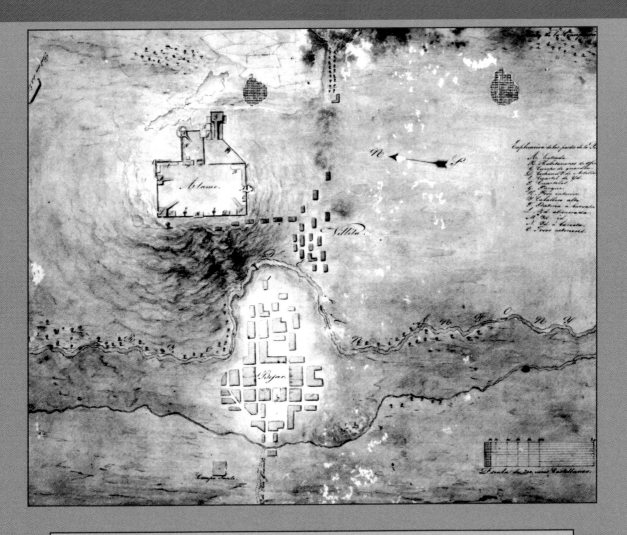

This map was prepared for Santa Anna by the chief military engineer, Colonel Ygnacio de Labastida, in March 1836. The Alamo is in the upper left, with San Antonio de Béxar below, on the other side of the San Antonio River. An arrow in the upper right of the map indicates that north is to the left. A list near the right edge of the map provides a key to the parts of the fortifications: A. Entrance; B. Officers' quarters; C. Guardhouse; D. Commander of Artillery; E. Barracks for same; F. Barracks; G. Magazine; H. Interior trench; I. High cavalier; J. Battery on carriage; L. Same, embrasure; M. Same, same; N. Same, on carriage; O. Exterior trenches. Across the bottom, Labastida has identified the map and even dedicated it: "Plan of the city of San Antonio de Béxar and Alamo fortification, compiled and drawn by Col. Ygnacio de Labastida, Chief of Engineers of the Army of the North, who dedicates it to the Most Excellent Señor Gen. Don Vicente Filisola, second in command of the same army." The map is now in the collection of the Center for American History at the University of Texas at Austin.

TEXAS
FOREVER!!

The usurper of the South has failed in his efforts to enslave the freemen of Texas.

The wives and daughters of Texas will be saved from the brutality of Mexican soldiers.

Now is the time to emigrate to the Garden of America.

A free passage, and all found, is offered at New Orleans to all applicants. Every settler receives a location of

EIGHT HUNDRED ACRES OF LAND.

On the 23d of February, a force of 1000 Mexicans came in sight of San Antonio, and on the 25th Gen. St. Anna arrived at that place with 2500 more men, and demanded a surrender of the fort held by 150 Texians, and on the refusal, he attempted to storm the fort, twice, with his whole force, but was repelled with the loss of 500 men, and the Americans lost none. Many of his troops, the liberals of Zacatecas, are brought on to Texas in irons and are urged forward with the promise of the women and plunder of Texas.

The Texian forces were marching to relieve St. Antonio, March the 2d. The Government of Texas is supplied with plenty of arms, ammunition, provisions, &c. &c.

This broadside was intended to attract volunteers to the Texas cause by inciting hatred of the Mexican army. Santa Anna and his troops are described in terms that make them sound like monsters. In case hatred of the Mexicans is not enough to persuade volunteers to join the fight, each settler is promised an enormous plot of land. There is no way to know how many people might have responded to the broadside. No printer's name and address appear on the broadside to tell where it was printed and who printed it. Since it mentions free passage from New Orleans, it seems likely that it was printed in that city, but there is no way to guess who the printer was. Since the broadside claims that reinforcements were on the way to the Alamo on March 2, it must have been printed after that date. This is the only known surviving copy of the broadside; it is part of the Broadside Collection in the Center for American History at the University of Texas at Austin. See page 57 for an excerpt.

Alamo, Travis was one of the first defenders to die. The Texans abandoned the walls and barricaded themselves inside the buildings. The Mexicans pursued them, and bloody hand-to-hand fighting followed. Bowie, who had fallen ill on February 24, was killed on his cot. Crockett died as well, though there are different stories about how he died. The battle lasted less than an hour and a half. Almost all the volunteers and regular army troops defending the Alamo died during the battle. The few who survived were executed immediately.

Though all the defenders died, there were survivors who were allowed to go free. Santa Anna gave safe passage, a blanket, and two dollars to each woman, child, and slave inside the Alamo. They carried word about the battle to the rest of Texas.

The first published account of the Battle of the Alamo appeared on March 24, 1836, in the *Telegraph & Texas Register*, published in San Felipe by Baker and Bordens, the same printers who had published the Texas Declaration of Independence. It is reproduced on page 40. The account, pieced together from different sources, included a list of those known to have been killed at the Alamo, with a promise from the publishers to print additional names as they became known.

Accounts of the battle by Mexican soldiers also exist. One of the best known is the memoir of Lieutenant Colonel José Enrique de la Peña, part of which is reproduced on page 41. Peña expressed his admiration for the courage of the Alamo defenders, with special praise for Travis. Travis, Peña wrote, "fought like a true soldier. Finally he died, but he died after having traded his life very dearly. None of his men died with greater heroism, and they all died. Travis behaved as a hero; one must do him justice." Peña's account of Crockett's death has created great

The importance that Texans attached to the fall of the Alamo can be judged by the language used in this account from the *Telegraph & Texas Register*. Already the Alamo's defenders were being elevated to legendary status—hailed as godlike—while the Mexican army was demonized. The narrative recounts how the defenders fought to the bitter end, "until life ebbed out through their numberless wounds and the enemy had conquered the fort, but not its brave, its matchless defenders: they perished, but they yielded not." The story proclaims that the defenders' deeds will always be remembered and will inspire future generations: "The darkness of death occupied the memorable Alamo, but recently so teeming with gallant spirits and filled with deeds of never-failing remembrance . . . Who would not be rather one of the Alamo heroes, than of the living of its merciless victors? Spirits of the mighty, though fallen! Honours and rest are with ye: the spark of immortality which animated your forms, shall brighten into a flame, and Texas, the whole world, shall hail ye like demi-gods of old, as founders of new actions, and as patterns for imitation!" See pages 57–58 for an additional excerpt from the article.

Lieutenant Colonel José Enrique de la Peña's manuscript was purchased by San Antonio businessman John Peace in Mexico in the early 1970s. He loaned it to the University of Texas at San Antonio, where it stayed until 1998. At that time, members of the Peace family took back the manuscript to offer it for sale at auction. Two Texas businessmen, Thomas Hicks and Charles Tate, purchased the manuscript and donated it to the Center for American History at the University of Texas at Austin, where it remains today. Because Peña's account of Crockett's death differs from the one most people accept, some people believe that Peña's story isn't true. Some even think that the manuscript may be a forgery. For a translation of an excerpt from the manuscript, see page 58.

controversy among modern historians. Most people believe that Crockett died during the battle, but Peña claimed that Crockett was one of the seven defenders who survived and was executed by Santa Anna.

CHAPTER 5

Following the fall of the Alamo, Sam Houston and the revolutionary army retreated, moving east across the Colorado River and finally camping near Columbia, Texas, on the Brazos River. Houston needed time to train his troops before they could face the Mexican army.

While Houston was getting his men ready to fight, he sent orders to James Fannin at Goliad, about eighty miles southeast of the Alamo, to retreat with his 500 soldiers. Unfortunately, several days passed before Fannin carried out Houston's order. By that time, it was too late. Santa Anna and his army caught up with Fannin's troops quickly. Rather than fight, Fannin surrendered. Santa Anna declared the Texas soldiers "pirates" and ordered them all executed.

AFTER THE ALAMO

When word of the massacre reached Houston's men, some of them fled with their families in an episode called the Runaway Scrape. On the orders of David G. Burnet, temporary president of the Republic of Texas, Houston took his remaining soldiers and headed after Santa Anna's troops. Houston's men caught up with the Mexican army on the San Jacinto River near Galveston Bay on April 20, 1836. On the afternoon of April 21, while the Mexican army enjoyed an afternoon siesta, Houston placed his men in position to attack. With cries of "Remember the Alamo!" and "Remember Goliad!," the Texas army charged the sleeping Mexicans. The bloody battle was even shorter than the fight at the Alamo had been. It lasted only eighteen minutes. When it was over, 630 Mexican soldiers had been killed and 730 had been taken prisoner. Only nine Texans were killed and thirty wounded.

With the victory in the Battle of San Jacinto, the Texans had won their independence. In September 1836, the first elections were held, and Sam Houston became the first elected president of the Republic of Texas.

A map of the United States from 1839 (pictured on the next page), with parts of surrounding countries, provides considerable information about the Republic of Texas at that time. Texas and its neighbor, Mexico, occupy the southwestern third of the map. The detailed map shows towns, rivers, lakes, and bays along the coast. The Alamo and San Antonio de Béxar are in the lower central part of the republic. Three years after Texas had won its independence, there were still few towns. Most of the land was owned by only a few men. The large tracts of land they owned are labeled "locations" on the map.

Having won its independence from Mexico, Texas was now free to pursue its ultimate goal—to become a part of the United States. However, many people in the U.S. Congress opposed accepting Texas as a state. They objected to the fact that slavery was legal in Texas at a time when many people in the United States were trying to end slavery. It took almost ten years, but finally Texas became part of the United States. On December 29, 1845, President James Polk signed the paper that made Texas the twenty-eighth state. Texas formally joined the United States on February 19, 1846.

In the years following the Battle of the Alamo, Texas achieved what it had sought. But what happened to the survivors and the families of the defenders? One of the most famous survivors was Angelina Dickinson, known as the Babe of the Alamo because

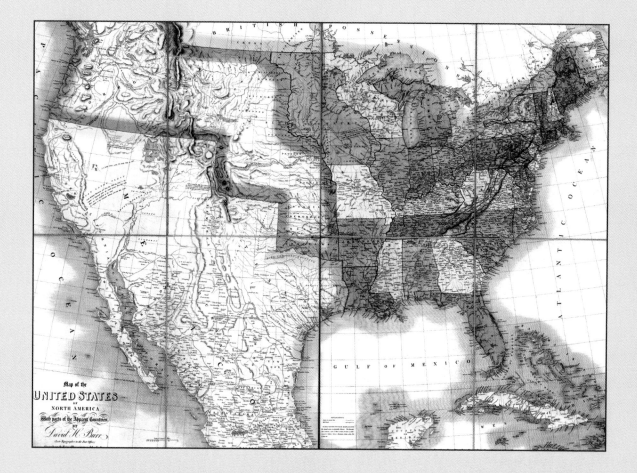

Map of the
UNITED STATES
OF
NORTH AMERICA
With parts of the Adjacent Countries.
BY
David H. Burr.

This map was made by David H. Burr (1803–1875), who made maps for both the U.S. Post Office and the U.S. House of Representatives. Burr was also a famous commercial cartographer, or mapmaker. This particular map was included in his *American Atlas*, which was published in London, England, in 1839, by J. Arrowsmith, a member of a famous English family of mapmakers. The map is an engraving, made by cutting lines into a metal plate with special tools. Ink was then rubbed into the lines and paper placed on the plate. When the plate and the paper were rolled through a press, the ink was transferred from the plate to the paper. Engraving allowed mapmakers to make very fine lines to record lots of detail, and it had been the preferred method for making maps since it was invented in the fifteenth century. This map is now in the Library of Congress.

she was only fifteen months old at the time of the battle. Her father was one of the defenders of the Alamo; both Angelina and her mother, Susanna, were among the survivors freed by the Mexican army. A portrait of Angelina is shown on page 46.

Angelina was born in 1834. Her life was sad and rather short. Her mother, Susanna, who was only twenty-two at the time of the Battle of the Alamo, was married four more times after being widowed at the Alamo. Some of these men abused Susanna. Two of the marriages ended in divorce, and Susanna was also widowed again. This troubled family life must have been very difficult for the young Angelina. At the age of seventeen, Angelina married John Maynard Griffith. The couple had three children, but the marriage ended in divorce after only six years. Angelina left her children with relatives and went to New Orleans, then to Galveston. She may have been married one or two more times there. When she was about thirty-five, she bled to death as the result of illness or injury.

The Republic of Texas awarded 640 acres of land to all the men who had fought for Texas's independence. The families of men who died in the war were entitled to claim that land. David Crockett's widow, Elizabeth, who with their four children had been left behind in Tennessee when Crockett set off to explore Texas, did not go to Texas to claim her 640 acres until 1853. Accompanied by three of her grown children and their families, Elizabeth spent almost a year looking for someone to accept her claim and make the necessary survey of the land she had chosen, near Acton, east of the Brazos River. Then she had to give 320 acres to the surveyor as payment. On the remaining 320 acres, her son Robert built log cabins for the extended family, and they farmed the land. Elizabeth continued to live there until her death in 1860 at the age of seventy-two.

Two stories about Angelina Dickinson at the time of the Alamo have been passed along over time. The first, which is probably true, tells that William Barret Travis gave her a ring that had been given to him by his sweetheart. Angelina later gave the ring to a man she loved. The second story, which may or may not be true, tells that Santa Anna was so charmed by the infant Angelina that he wanted to adopt her. The only source for the second story is Angelina's mother, Susanna, who told many stories about the Battle of the Alamo that are now known to be untrue. This undated photo of Angelina, taken by an unknown photographer, gives an idea of what she looked like but doesn't provide much information about her personality. The stiff pose and unsmiling face were normal for photographs from this period. Subjects were required to sit without moving for a long time in order to allow enough light to enter the camera to make the picture. To help people hold still, they were seated in a chair with a special device behind their head to keep it in place. They didn't smile because it was too difficult to hold a smile for a long time. Probably taken sometime between 1855 and Angelina's death around 1870, this photo is now in the Center for American History at the University of Texas at Austin.

No. 6127   **PUBLIC DEBT**   Second Class, "B."

OF THE

LATE REPUBLIC OF TEXAS.

This is to Certify, That *David Crockett dec'd for heirs* has, under the provisions of An Act of the **Legislature of the State of Texas,** entitled An Act to extend the provisions of "An Act to provide for ascertaining the Debt of the late Republic of Texas," approved February 7, 1853, filed with the **Auditor and Comptroller,** *claim for Service at the Alamo in 1836*

amounting to *Twenty four* Dollars; which is sufficiently authenticated to authorize the auditing of the same under the laws of the late Republic of Texas. Said claim, according to the data before us, is worth *Twenty four* Dollars, in par funds, as having been at that rate so available to the Government.

In Testimony Whereof, We have hereunto set our hands and affixed our seals of office, at Austin, this *2nd* day of *December* A. D. 1854.

Samuel Sherwood Comptroller.

Jno. M. Swisher Auditor.

The Republic of Texas made grants of 640 acres each to the men who fought in Texas's war for independence. By the time Elizabeth Crockett arrived to claim the grant owed to her late husband, David, the Republic of Texas no longer existed. It was now the state of Texas. However, the state still honored claims people made for goods and services (such as military service) that they had provided to Texas when it was a republic, as long as they could prove that those claims were true. To pay the claims, the state of Texas issued Public Debt Certificates, which stated at the top that the certificates were intended to pay a public debt left over from the time when Texas was a republic. The certificates said that the person named was entitled to receive payment from the state (the "public") in the amount listed. The payments were always given in terms of dollars, even if the person was to be paid in land, as Elizabeth was. According to this certificate, Crockett's service at the Alamo had entitled him to $24.00 in payment. Like all legal documents, these certificates were written in formal legal jargon that was far removed from everyday language. This certificate now belongs to the Texas State Library and Archives Commission.

CHAPTER 6

The legend of the Alamo that had begun to take shape in the first published account of the battle in the *Telegraph & Texas Register* on March 24, 1836, continued to grow. Not always based on accurate information, the legend took the real men who had defended the Alamo and turned them into larger-than-life heroes whose deeds exceeded anything that mortals could accomplish. The defenders and the battle itself became symbols of an eternal struggle for liberty shared by all humanity. In one sense, the legend has given the Alamo defenders a kind of immortality. In another sense, it has obscured a deeper understanding and appreciation of the real flesh-and-blood men who fought and died at the fort.

THE LEGEND OF THE ALAMO

After the fall of the Alamo, the fort was in ruins. The Republic of Texas had no use for it. In 1841, the republic returned control of the Alamo to the Catholic Church. By this time, the Alamo had become a sort of tourist attraction.

Thomas Falconer, an English lawyer and adventurer, left a visual record of the Alamo as it appeared when he visited it on April 22, 1841. Falconer kept a diary of his travels in Texas, and in it he included a drawing (seen on page 49) of the ruined front of the Alamo church. In the lower-left corner, Falconer wrote, "Entrance to the Church, within the Alamo at Bexar, Texas – April. 22. 1841 —".

Entrance of the Church, within the Alamo at Bexas. Texas –
April 22. 1841 –

Thomas Falconer (1805–1882) began practicing law in England in 1823. In 1840, he decided to immigrate to the Republic of Texas and set sail for the United States on October 20. His ship landed at Boston, Massachusetts, and from there he headed for the Texas capital, Austin. His journey took him through San Antonio, where he visited the Alamo and made this sketch. When Falconer arrived in Austin in May 1841, he heard about the plans for the Texan Santa Fe expedition, which was to explore the still largely unknown lands of western Texas and beyond. Attracted by the adventure, he persuaded Texas president Mirabeau B. Lamar to allow him to accompany the expedition as historian and scientific observer. The detailed account of the expedition in Falconer's diary provides the only surviving record of episodes such as the attack by the Kiowa Indians on the group. The diary was published as an appendix to the 1856 edition of *Narrative of the Texan Santa Fe Expedition* by George Wilkins Kendall, a member of the expedition. The original diary is in the Beinecke Rare Book and Manuscript Library at Yale University.

Neither the caption nor the image—painted in a soft ink wash—conveys a sense of the bloody battle that took place there. The church is presented as an interesting architectural ruin. Such ruins appealed to the romantic imagination of the time and had become so popular that some wealthy people in England actually had fake ruins built on their estates. Falconer's interest in the architecture of the church is evident in his attention to the elaborate entrance, which is more carefully painted than the rest of the building. Falconer was so concerned with getting the entrance details correct that he practiced painting the arch above the doorway in the lower-right corner of the page.

In 1849, eight years after Falconer made his sketch of the Alamo, a photograph of the church was taken. Shown on page 51, this is the earliest known photograph of the Alamo and the only one taken before a reconstruction in 1850 added the curved top above the entrance that is still there today. This photograph is also the earliest datable photograph taken in Texas, and that says a great deal about how important a symbol the Alamo had become. Out of all the possible subjects that were considered at the time to be suitable material for photography—towns, landscapes, and important people—the unknown photographer chose the Alamo.

The photographer eliminated the surrounding area from the picture so that the viewer's attention is focused on the Alamo itself. It is almost like a portrait of the church. Three people stand or sit in front of the building, and when their size is compared to the size of the church, the viewer may be surprised to discover that the building is not as large in reality as it has grown to be in legend.

In 1870, Texas governor Edmund Davis chose painter Henry Arthur McArdle to make large oil paintings on canvas showing

This photograph of the Alamo is a daguerreotype, an early type of photograph. To make this image, a copper plate was coated with silver and treated with chemicals to make it sensitive to light. The plate was then put in a camera and the picture was taken. Daguerreotypes were admired for their incredible detail. Unfortunately, light reflected from the silver-coated plate, making it difficult to see the image clearly. The surface was also easily damaged, so daguerreotypes were kept in protective frames, like the one shown here. In addition, each daguerreotype was unique; it could not be duplicated. This daguerreotype was purchased by Texas governor Dolph Briscoe and his wife in 1993 for the Center for American History at the University of Texas at Austin.

battles and heroes of the Texas war for independence. One of the paintings, titled *Dawn at the Alamo*, was to show the Battle of the Alamo. McArdle took great care to gather accurate information about the event before he began painting. He researched what the landscape around the Alamo had looked like, what uniforms had been worn by the soldiers, and what equipment each army had used. McArdle also looked for portraits or photographs of the famous people involved so that he could make accurate likenesses of them in his painting. McArdle even contacted General Santa Anna, who was still living, to ask if he could provide any additional information about the battle. Santa Anna's reply, which still survives, consisted mostly of explaining why he had found it necessary to kill all of the Alamo's defenders.

In spite of McArdle's extensive research and apparent concern with accuracy, his painting of the Battle of the Alamo is more an interpretation of the event than a factual portrayal of it. He made many choices in how to paint the scene that made the defenders look particularly heroic and the Mexican soldiers look particularly villainous. McArdle used light to draw special attention to William Barret Travis, David Crockett, and James Bowie, and presented them in heroic poses. He even placed a pale Bowie in the thick of the battle. This incident was a complete fabrication on McArdle's part; Bowie had been too ill to join the fight and had been killed while lying on his cot. The artist also made the three heroes handsome.

In contrast, the Mexican soldiers have coarse, heavy, exaggerated features and assume poses that are definitely not heroic. As Travis, standing tall, faces Mexican soldiers coming over the wall and shoots them, one sneaks up unseen behind him, preparing to stab him with a bayonet—this is the act of a coward, not a hero.

Another painting McArdle did for the Texas governor showed the San Jacinto battle. Like his painting of the Battle of the Alamo, McArdle's *Battle of San Jacinto* glorifies the Texas soldiers. Both paintings are impressively large: *Dawn at the Alamo* is about seven feet tall and twelve feet wide, and the *Battle of San Jacinto* is about eight feet tall and fourteen feet wide. Today, both paintings hang in the Senate Chamber in the Texas Capitol, where they teach thousands of people every year about the legend of the Alamo, though not about the real history.

After Texas became part of the United States in 1846, control over the Alamo changed hands many times. First, the U.S. government decided that the Alamo belonged to the United States, not the Catholic Church, and began using it as a military supply depot in 1848. Confederate troops occupied the fort during the Civil War. After the North won the Civil War, the U.S. government again took over the Alamo and continued to use it until 1876. The Catholic Church then took control of the Alamo once again.

This handwritten deed of sale for the Alamo is a formal legal document that uses the language that is standard in all deeds and that is still in use today. Such documents give the name of the seller, the name of the buyer, and the surveyed measurements of the land being purchased. They also list any structures on the land. There is nothing in the language of the deed to indicate the enormous symbolic importance attached to the Alamo. The only clue to its importance lies in the sale price, which is also noted in the deed: the state of Texas paid the Catholic Church $20,000, a staggering sum in 1883, for the fort that legend had turned into a shrine to all who had fought and died to win independence for Texas. For a transcription of an excerpt of the deed, see page 58.

In 1882, the Catholic bishop for San Antonio, John Claud Neraz, decided to sell the Alamo to raise money for other projects and offered the state of Texas the chance to buy it. On April 23, 1883, the Texas legislature passed a bill authorizing the purchase of the Alamo and placing it under the care of the city of San Antonio. Bishop Neraz's offer to sell the Alamo to the state and the deed of sale both survive.

The Alamo remained in the care of the city of San Antonio until January 25, 1905, when the Texas legislature passed a resolution ordering the governor to transfer control of the Alamo to the Daughters of the Republic of Texas.

The Daughters of the Republic of Texas was formed in 1891 as an organization for women who were the direct descendants of the men and women who founded the Republic of Texas. The members work to make sure that the people who struggled to make Texas free are not forgotten. They encourage historical research involving the earliest Texas documents and promote the teaching of Texas history in the public schools.

Today, anyone can visit the Alamo and see the historical documents and objects there. The agreement between the state and the Daughters requires that the Daughters take care of the Alamo church and the surrounding grounds, and that they charge people no admission fee to visit the Alamo. However, there have been disagreements between the Daughters and the Texas governor's office about restoration of the Alamo. There continue to be disputes about who will have the privilege of caring for the Alamo and about how historical information will be presented there. Even in modern times, it seems, the history of the Alamo is one of struggle.

PRIMARY SOURCE TRANSCRIPTIONS

Page 15: Excerpt of Letter from Provincial Deputy Aldasoro to Texas Governor Martínez

TRANSLATION FROM SPANISH
Señor Governor D. Antonio Martínez
Monterrey January 17 1821

Dear Sir:
In all the meetings we have had, I have born in mind the needs of the province, and as I offered to you and its population, to help, with all my effort, listening to this Superior Chief of the Provincial Government, to secure the move of the neighbors of "Misuri," in accordance with your desires. I have tried, with all my effort as I said, to dispose the government to accede to the request of the interested person. In this same mail this permission is granted; and anyway congratulations on your management of this.

Page 22: Excerpt of Letter from General Martín Perfecto de Cos to Political Chief at Béxar

TRANSLATION FROM SPANISH
You will provide in this matter all the boost it deserves for a better outcome, and with confidence I have the great pleasure to reinforce my affection for you.
God and freedom. [???]
October 17. 1835.
Martín Perfecto de Cos

Departmental Political Chief

Page 25: Excerpt from the Proclamation of Sam Houston

TRANSCRIPTION
     The services of five thousand volunteers will be accepted. By the first of March next, we must meet the enemy with an army worthy of our cause, and which will reflect honor upon freemen. Our habitations must be defended; the sanctity of our hearths and firesides must be preserved from pollution. Liberal Mexicans will unite with us. Our countrymen in the field have presented an example worthy of imitation. Generous and brave hearts from a land of freedom have joined our standard before Bejar. They have, by their heroism and valor called forth the admiration of their comrades in arms, and have reflected additional honor on the land of their birth.
     Let the brave rally to our standard!

SAM. HOUSTON,
Commander-in-chief of the Army.

By order,
          George W. Poe,
               Acting Adjutant-General.

Page 33: William Barret Travis's Letter from the Alamo

TRANSCRIPTION
Commandancy of the Alamo—
Bejar, Fby 24th 1836—

To the People of Texas & all Americans in the world—

Fellow citizens & compatriots—
I am besieged, by a thousand or more of the Mexicans under Santa Anna—I have sustained a continual Bombardment & cannonade for 24 hours & have not lost a man—The enemy has demanded a surrender at discretion, otherwise, the garrison are to be put to the sword, if the fort is taken—I have answered the demand with a cannon shot, & our flag still waves proudly from the walls—I shall never surrender or retreat. Then, I call on you in the name of Liberty, of patriotism & everything dear to the American character, to come to our aid.

Page 35: Excerpt from the Texas Declaration of Independence

TRANSCRIPTION
When long after the spirit of the constitution has departed, moderation is at length so far lost by those in power, that even the semblance of freedom is removed, and the forms themselves of the constitution discontinued, and so far from their petitions and remonstrances being regarded, the agents who bear them are thrown into dungeons, and mercenary armies sent forth to force a new government upon them at the point of the bayonet.

When, in consequence of such acts of malfeasance and abdication on the part of the government, anarchy prevails, and civil society is dissolved into its original elements, in such a crisis, the first law of nature, the right of self preservation, the inherent and inalienable right of the people to appeal to first principles, and take their political affairs into their own hands in extreme cases, enjoins it as a right towards themselves and a sacred obligation to their posterity to abolish such government, and create another in its stead, calculated to rescue them from impending dangers, and to secure their welfare and happiness.

Page 38: Excerpt from the TEXAS FOREVER!! Broadside

TRANSCRIPTION
TEXAS FOREVER!! The usurper of the South has failed in his efforts to enslave the freemen of Texas. The wives and daughters of Texas will be saved from the brutality of Mexican soldiers. Now is the time to emigrate to the Garden of America. A free passage, and all found, is offered at New Orleans to all applicants. Every settler receives a location of EIGHT HUNDRED ACRES OF LAND. On the 23d of February, a force of 1000 Mexicans came in sight of San Antonio, and on the 25th Gen St. Anna arrived at that place with 2500 more men, and demanded a surrender of the fort held by 150 Texians, and on the refusal, he attempted to storm the fort, twice, with his whole force, but was repelled with the loss of 500 men, and the Americans lost none.

Page 40: Excerpt from "More Particulars Respecting the Fall of the Alamo"

TRANSCRIPTION
This event, so lamentable, and yet so glorious to Texas, is of such deep interest and excites so much our feelings that we shall never cease to celebrate it, and regret that we are not acquainted with the names of all those who fell in that Fort, that we might publish them, and thus consecrate to future ages the memory of our heroes who perished at the Thermopylae of Texas. Such examples are bright ones, and should be held up as mirrors, that by reflection, we may catch the spirit and learn to fashion our own behaviour. The list of names inserted below, was furnished

by Mr. Jas. W. Smith, and Mr. Navon, and as we obtain more we will publish them. To Mr. Smith, who has rendered good service to Texas, and to Judge Ponton are we indebted for the particulars, as communicated to them by Mrs. Dickinson, who was in the "Alamo" during the siege and assault.

Page 41: Pages from Peña Manuscript Describing Deaths of Travis and Crockett

TRANSLATION FROM SPANISH

Some seven men had survived the general carnage and, under the protection of General Castrillón, they were brought before Santa Anna. Among them was one of great stature, well proportioned, with regular features, in whose face there was the imprint of adversity, but in whom one also noticed a degree of resignation and nobility that did him honor. He was the naturalist David Crockett, well known in North America for his unusual adventures, who had undertaken to explore the country and who, finding himself in Béjar at the very moment of surprise, had taken refuge in the Alamo, fearing that his status as a foreigner might not be respected. Santa Anna answered Castrillón's intervention in Crockett's behalf with a gesture of indignation and, addressing himself to the sappers, the troops closest to him, ordered his execution. The commanders and officers were outraged at this action and did not support the order, hoping that once the fury of the moment had blown over these men would be spared; but several officers who were around the president and who, perhaps, had not been present during the moment of danger, became noteworthy by an infamous deed, surpassing the soldiers in cruelty. They thrust themselves forward, in order to flatter their commander, and with swords in hand, fell upon these unfortunate, defenseless men just as a tiger leaps upon his prey. Though tortured before they were killed, these unfortunates died without complaining and without humiliating themselves before their torturers.

Page 52: Excerpt from Letter from Santa Anna to Henry A. McArdle

TRANSLATION FROM SPANISH

Dear Sir:

In response to your favor of the 4th of January, I have to say that in regard to the capture or restoration of the fortress of the Alamo, in April 1836 there is but little I can add to what was said in my official dispatches, and what was common knowledge. Notwithstanding, for your satisfaction, I will add that, that conflict of arms was bloody, because the chief Travis, who commanded the forces of the Alamo, would not enter into any settlement, and his responses were insulting, which made it imperative to assault the fort before it could be reinforced by Samuel Houston who was marching to its aid with respectable forces. The obstinacy of Travis and his soldiers was the cause of the death of the whole of them, for not one would surrender. The struggle lasted more than two hours, and until the ramparts were resolutely scaled by Mexican soldiers.

Page 54: Excerpt from the Deed, Sale of Alamo Church to the State of Texas

TRANSCRIPTION

State of Texas
County of Travis
Know all men by these presents that the Catholic Church of the Diocese of San Antonio in the State of Texas acting by and through John C. Neraz, Catholic Bishop of said diocese, its only authorized agent, and trustee for the property hereinafter described, for and in consideration of Twenty Thousand Dollars to it in hand paid by John Ireland, Governor of the State of Texas, the receipt whereof is hereby acknowledged, has granted, bargained, sold, released and conveyed, and by these presents does grant, bargain, sell, release and convey unto the State of Texas all of that tract or parcel of land situated and lying in the City of San Antonio, County of Bexar and State of Texas and described by metes and bounds as follows.

GLOSSARY

almanac An annual publication containing general information about someone or something.

Anglo A short form of the Spanish word *angloamericano*, applied to white people in North America who are not of Spanish descent.

barricade To put up barriers to block an enemy's advance.

buffer A zone separating two groups from each other.

commission An appointment to military rank and authority.

dictator Someone who rules with absolute power.

equestrian Showing a person on horseback, as in a painting or statue.

exaggerate To distort something, often in an unflattering way, by making it larger than normal.

fabrication A lie or falsehood.

glorify To elevate someone or something by bestowing lavish honor and praise.

hilt The handle of a sword.

land speculator A person who buys land hoping to sell it to someone else for a much higher price.

massacre The killing of a large number of people, especially when it seems unjustified.

militia A group of citizens who are not soldiers but who have been organized for military service.

propaganda The spreading of ideas and information, not necessarily true, to help one's own cause or to hurt an enemy's cause.

reinforcements Additional soldiers to increase the number of soldiers at a specific location.

scabbard A long, narrow case for a sword.

siege A military blockade around a city or fort to force it to surrender.

skirmish A minor battle in a war.

FOR MORE INFORMATION

Web Sites

Due to the changing nature of Internet links, the Rosen Publishing Group, Inc., has developed an online list of Web sites related to the subject of this book. This site is updated regularly. Please use this link to access the list:

http://www.rosenlinks.com/psah/alam/

FOR FURTHER READING

Chariton, Wallace O. *Exploring the Alamo Legends*. Plano, TX: Wordware Publishing, 1992.

Groneman, Bill, and Paul Andrew Hutton. *Eyewitness to the Alamo*. Rev. ed. Plano, TX: Republic of Texas Press, 2001.

Hardin, Stephen L. *The Alamo 1836: Santa Anna's Texas Campaign*. Oxford, UK: Osprey Publishing Co., 2001.

Hatch, Thom. *Encyclopedia of the Alamo and the Texas Revolution*. Jefferson, NC: McFarland & Company, 1999.

Matovina, Timothy M. *The Alamo Remembered: Tejano Accounts and Perspectives*. Austin, TX: University of Texas Press, 1995.

Peña, José Enrique de la. *With Santa Anna in Texas: A Personal Narrative of the Revolution*. College Station, TX: Texas A&M University Press, 1997.

Petite, Mary Deborah. *1836: Facts About the Alamo and the Texas War for Independence*. Cambridge, MA: Da Capo Press, 1999.

# BIBLIOGRAPHY

Catlin, George. "Letters and Notes on the Manners, Customs, and Conditions of North American Indians." Retrieved November 16, 2001 (http://www.xmission.com/~drudy/mtman/html/catlin/letter42.html).

Daughters of the Republic of Texas. "The Alamo." Retrieved November 16, 2001 (http://www.thealamo.org).

Kyle, Robert. "Rare Jim Bowie Portrait Goes Home to Texas." From *Maine Antique Digest*. August 2001. Retrieved November 20, 2001 (http://www.maineantiquedigest.com/articles/bow10801.htm).

McKeehan, Wallace L. "Sons of Dewitt Colony Texas." Retrieved November 30, 2001 (http://www.tamu.edu/ccbn/dewitt/dewitt.htm).

Moore, R. E. "The Texas Comanches." Retrieved December 20, 2001 (http://www.texasindians.com/comanche.htm).

Paesani, Mario. "Birth of the Lone Star State." 1996. Retrieved November 16, 2001 (http://members.tripod.com/aries46/lonestar.htm).

Panhandle-Plains Historical Museum. "Texas Art Teaches Texas History." Retrieved December 21, 2001 (http://www.panhandleplains.org/script.html).

Texas State Historical Association. "The Handbook of Texas Online." Retrieved November 16–December 20, 2001 (http://www.tsha.utexas.edu/handbook/online).

Texas State Library and Archives Commission. Retrieved November 30, 2001 (http://www.tsl.state.tx.us).

University of Pennsylvania Library. "Keffer Collection of Sheet Music, ca. 1790–1895: Philadelphia Lithographers: George Lehman (d. 1870)." Retrieved November 29, 2001 (http://www.library.upenn.edu/special/keffer/lehman.html).

The West Film Project and WETA. "New Perspectives on the West." Retrieved November 19, 2001 (http://www.pbs.org/weta/thewest/people).

INDEX

RIMARY SOURCE LIST

Page 10: Painting by George Catlin, 1834, called *Little Spaniard*. It is currently housed at the Smithsonian American Art Museum in Washington, D.C.

Page 12: Lithograph of Apache warrior on horse from 1828 by Claudio Linati. It is currently housed at the New York Public Library in New York City, New York.

Page 15: Letter from Ambrosio María de Aldasoro to Governor Antonio Martínez, 1821. It is currently housed at the Béxar Archives in the Center for American History at the University of Texas at Austin.

Page16: Portrait of Stephen F. Austin from 1833 by William Howard. It is currently part of the James Perry Bryan Papers at the Center for American History at the University of Texas at Austin.

Page 17: Map probably drawn by Stephen Austin in 1822. It is currently housed at the Library of Congress in Washington, D.C.

Page 20: Engraved portrait of Santa Anna by W. H. Dodd from the 1830s. It is currently housed at the Center for American History at the University of Texas at Austin.

Page 22: Letter from General Martín Perfecto de Cos to José Ángel Navarro, 1835. It is currently housed at the Béxar Archives at the Center for American History at the University of Texas at Austin.

Page 23: Drawing by José Juan Sánchez Navarro of the Alamo from 1835 to 1836, housed at the Beinecke Library at Yale University in New Haven, Connecticut.

Page 24: Portrait of Sam Houston, circa 1836, by Louis Antoine Collas. It is currently housed at the Sam Houston Memorial Museum at Sam Houston State University in Huntsville, Texas.

Page 25: Broadside of Army of Texas by Baker and Bordens in San Felipe de Austin, 1835. It is currently housed at the Texas State Library and Archives in Austin, Texas.

Page 27: Lithograph of David Crockett by Samuel Stillman Osgood, circa 1833. It is currently housed at the Center for American History at the University of Texas at Austin.

Page 29: Portrait of James Bowie by either George Peter Alexander Healy or William Edward West, painted sometime between 1820 and 1836. It is currently housed at the Capitol Historical Artifact Collection of the Texas State Preservation Board in Austin, Texas.

Page 33: Letter by William Barret Travis written in 1836. It is currently housed at the Texas State Library and Archives Commission in Austin, Texas.

Page 35: Broadside of the Texas Declaration of Independence, 1836. It is currently housed at the Center for American History at the University of Texas at Austin.

Page 37: Map by Colonel Ygnacio de Labastida, 1836. It is currently housed at the Center for American History at the University of Texas at Austin.

Page 38: Broadside urging Texans to fight. The artist and printer are unknown, but it might have been printed in New Orleans, circa 1836. It is currently housed in the Broadside Collection in the Center for American History at the University of Texas at Austin.

Page 40: *Telegraph & Texas Register*, 1836. It is currently housed at the Center for American History at the University of Texas at Austin.

Page 41: Manuscript by José Enrique de la Peña. It is currently housed at the Center for American History at the University of Texas at Austin.

Page 44: Map of United States by David H. Burr, 1839. It is currently housed at the Library of Congress in Washington, D.C.

Page 46: Photo of Angelina Dickinson, circa 1855–1870. It is currently housed at the Center for American History at the University of Texas at Austin.

Page 47: The Republic of Texas Public Debt Certificate, 1854. It is currently housed at the Texas State Library and Archives Commission in Austin, Texas.

Page 49: Sketch of the Alamo by Thomas Falconer, 1841. It is currently housed at the Beinecke Rare Book and Manuscript Library at Yale University in New Haven, Connecticut.

Page 51: Daguerreotype of the Alamo in 1849. It is owned by Dolph Briscoe and his wife, Janey Briscoe.

Page 52: Letter from General Santa Anna to Henry Arthur McArdle, 1874. It is currently housed at the Texas State Library and Archives Commission in Austin, Texas.

Page 54: Deed of sale for the Alamo. It is currently housed at the Texas State Library and Archives Commission in Austin, Texas.

About the Author

Janey Levy has a Ph.D. in art history from the University of Kansas. She has taught art history classes at several colleges and universities, published articles and essays on art history, and curated two art exhibits. Ms. Levy and her family, including two dogs, two cats, and assorted fish, live in the countryside near Buffalo, New York. She has written several books for the Rosen Publishing Group's classroom division, including *Primary Sources in Early American History.*

Photo Credits

Cover © Hulton/Archive/Getty Images; p. 1 © Corbis; pp. 10, 27 © Smithsonian American Art Museum, Washington, DC/Art Resources; p. 12 © New York Public Library; pp. 15, 16, 20, 22, 35, 37, 38, 40, 41, 46, 51, 52, 54 © Center for American History, University of Texas, Austin, TX; pp. 17, 23, 29, 44, 49 © Library of Congress; p. 24 © Sam Houston Memorial Museum at Sam Houston State University; pp. 25, 33, 47 © Texas State Library & Archives Commission.

Editor

Annie Sommers

Design

Nelson Sá